Dave Barry's
Book of
Bad Songs

Dave Barry's Book of Bad Songs

Dave Barry

**Andrews McMeel
Publishing**

Kansas City

Library of Congress Cataloging-in-Publication Data

Barry, Dave.
    Dave Barry's book of bad songs / by Dave Barry.
       p. cm.
    ISBN 0-8362-1443-9 (pbk.)
    1. Popular music—Humor.   I. Title.
  ML65.B3   1997
  782.42164—dc20   96-36790
                                                     CIP
                                                     MN

Design by Mauna Eichner

Information regarding excerpted lyrics can be found in Credits on page 89.

*This book is dedicated
To whoever put the bomp
In the bomp ba-bomp ba-bomp*

"Wo wo wo"

"Feelings"
MORRIS ALBERT

"Wo wo wo wo"

"My Love"
PAUL McCARTNEY

"Wo-o-o-o-o-o-o"

"What's New Pussycat"
AS SUNG BY TOM JONES

"I said na
Na na na na
Na na na na
Na na na
Na na na
Na na na na"

"Land of 1,000 Dances"

Cannibal and the Headhunters

Contents

WARNING!

Do not read this book. It will put bad songs into your brain.

Actually, that statement is not quite accurate: The bad songs are already *in* your brain. Your brain has an amazing capacity to remember bad songs. This is because of the way your brain assigns memory priority, as shown in this chart:

Memory Priority Assigned by Your Brain	Type of Information
Low	Your ATM number; your blood type; the location of your car keys; names of people you have known for years.
Medium	Totally useless information you learned in fifth grade, such as the capital of Vermont.[1]
High	Commercial jingles for products that as far as you know no longer exist, such as Bosco.[2]
Ultimate Highest	Songs you really, really hate.

---

[1] Montpelier.

[2] "I LOVE Bosco! That's the drink for me! Momma puts it in my milk," etc.

So I can guarantee you that many, if not most, of the bad songs discussed in this book are already festering somewhere in your brain. The good news is, most of the time these songs are dormant. The bad news is, every now and then something will wake one of the songs up, and you will have a hard time making it go back to sleep.

For example, you'll be enjoying a pleasant day at home, reading a book, when suddenly somebody—perhaps a trusted family member—will, out of the clear blue, hum just a few notes of the song "(I Never Promised You a) Rose Garden." Since this is a song that you have detested from the first instant you heard it, your brain has assigned it a prime memory location. The song immediately wakes up and starts echoing in your skull so that no matter how hard you try to focus on your book, all you can hear is that woman's smarmy voice singing

> *I beg your PARdon...*
> *I never promised you a ROSE garden!*

And since this is the only part of the song your brain remembers, it repeats it over and over and

OVER AND OVER AND OVER, sometimes for *days*, until you want to commit suicide by driving off a cliff, except you can't remember where you left your car keys.

That is the danger posed by this book. This book lists *dozens* and *dozens* of songs that are so bad they make "(I Never Promised You a) Rose Garden" sound, in terms of musical quality, like "The Messiah."[3] If you keep reading, you're going to have all *kinds* of bad songs waking up and creeping around inside your brain, refusing to die, just like the corpses in the movie *The Night of the Living Dead*, except all the corpses did was eat innocent civilians, which is not nearly as bad as causing innocent civilians to hum "A Horse with No Name."

You may ask: "Dave, if this book is such a bad thing, why on Earth should I buy it? What can I do with a book that I'm not supposed to read?"

The answer is: You can give it to somebody you don't like. This book is an *extremely* powerful psychological weapon; it can immobilize even the most powerful intellect.

---

[3] "The Messiah" was a 1973 hit by Three Dog Night.

Suppose you're a candidate for a big promotion, but the other candidate is a coworker who happens to be very smart. All you have to do is surreptitiously leave this book on his desk (after first tearing out this warning section). After he reads just a few pages, he will have the brain functionality of an ashtray. He'll be staring at important work papers, trying desperately to read and comprehend them, but he will be unable to do this because he will hear Gary Puckett's voice inside his brain, howling:

> YOUNG *girl, get out of my mind!*
> *My love for you is way out of line!*

His career will be over. The end will come when he tries to make an important presentation, and he blurts out, in front of the corporation's top-ranking officers, that he is too sexy for his shirt.

That is the kind of weapon this book is; that is the power it has. Use it wisely.

And whatever you do, *don't turn the next page.*

I'm Really Serious. Do *Not* Turn the Page. You *Will* Regret It.

Okay, I see I'm going to have to use drastic measures to get your attention. I didn't want to have to do this to you, but it's for your own good:

> *Muskrat Suzy*
> *Muskrat Sam*
> *Do the jitterbug*
> *Out in muskrat land...*

Had enough? I'm warning you, it's going to get worse! I haven't even mentioned Barry Manilow yet! Let alone Bobby Goldsboro! Turn back now, while you still have some, umm, some

> *Floatin' like the heavens above, looks like*

OH NO! I CAN'T STOP MYSELF! I CAN'T STOP

♪ MUSKRAT ♫
LOOOOOOOOVE

Too late.

Introduction

Why You Should Not Blame Me
for This Book

T his book, like so many of the unpleasant things that we encounter as we go through life, is Neil Diamond's fault. Here's what happened:

One day back in 1992, I was doing what I am almost always doing, namely, trying to write a newspaper column despite the fact that I have nothing important, or even necessarily true, to say.

In this particular column, I was complaining about the fact that they never play any good songs on the radio. When I say "good songs," I of course mean "songs that I personally like." For example, I happen to love "Twist and Shout" as performed by the Isley Brothers. As far as I am concerned, oldies-format radio stations should be required by federal law to play this song at least once per hour.

But they hardly ever play it. Instead, they play "Love Child" as performed by Diana Ross and the Supremes, which is a song that you can listen to only so many times. And when I say "only so many times," I mean "once." And if they ever do play "Twist and Shout," for some bizarre reason they play the Beatles' version, which, according to mathematical calculations performed by powerful university computers, is only $\frac{1}{10,000}$ as good as the Isley Brothers' version.

So anyway, in this column I was ranting about songs that I don't particularly care for, and I happened to bring up Neil Diamond. I didn't say I hate *all* Neil Diamond songs; I actually like some of them.[1] Here's exactly what I wrote:

> It would not trouble me if the radio totally ceased playing ballad-style songs by Neil Diamond. I realize that many of you are huge Neil Diamond fans, so let me stress that, in matters of musical taste, everybody is entitled to an opinion, and yours is wrong. Consider the song "I Am, I Said," wherein Neil, with great emotion, sings:
>
> > *I am, I said*
> > *To no one there*
> > *And no one heard at all*
> > *Not even the chair.*
>
> What kind of line is that? Is Neil telling us he's *surprised* that the chair didn't hear him?

---

[1] For example, I really like "Play Me," especially the part where Neil sings, "Song she sang to me; song she brang to me."

Maybe he expected the chair to say, "Whoa, I heard THAT." My guess is that Neil was really desperate to come up with something to rhyme with "there," and he had already rejected "So I ate a pear," "Like Smokey the Bear," and "There were nits in my hair."

So that was what I wrote: A restrained, fair, and totally unbiased analysis of this song. Who could possibly be offended?

Well. You think Salman Rushdie got into trouble. It turns out that Neil Diamond has a great many *serious* fans out there, and virtually every one of them took the time to send me an extremely hostile, spittle-flecked letter. In a subsequent column, I combined the key elements of these letters into one all-purpose irate–Neil Diamond–fan letter, as follows:

Dear Pukenose:

Just who the hell do you think you are to blah blah a great artist like Neil blah more than twenty gold records blah blah how many gold records do YOU have, you scumsucking wad of blah I personally have attended 1,794 of Neil's concerts blah blah What about "Love on the Rocks," huh? What about "Cracklin' Rosie"?

blah blah If you had ONE-TENTH of Neil's talent blah blah so I listened to "Heart Light" forty times in a row and the next day the cyst was GONE and the doctor said he had never seen such a rapid blah blah What about "Play Me"? What about "Song Sung Blah"? Cancel my subscription, if I have one.

The thing is, I got at least as many letters, just as strongly worded, *attacking* Neil Diamond. But that was just the beginning: I got a whole lot *more* letters from people who wanted to complain about other songs that they hated to hear on the radio. And these people were *angry*. These people were advocating the use of tactical nuclear weapons against the next radio station to play, for example, "American Pie."

I have, in my twenty years as a newspaper columnist, written about many vitally important issues—politics, the economy, foreign policy, mutant constipated worms, etc.—and none of these topics has ever stirred up so much passion in the readers as the issue of bad songs. People were stopping me on the street, grabbing me by the shirt, and, with cold fury in their eyes, saying things like: "You know that song about the piña coladas? I HATE THAT SONG! I HATE IT!!"

So I realized that I had tapped into a throbbing artery of emotion. I realized that Americans—who are so often accused of not being interested in or informed about the issues—care very deeply about song badness. I also realized that, by probing deeper into this subject, I had a chance to do something that could provide a truly significant benefit to the human race; namely, I could get an easy column out of it.

And thus I decided to conduct the Bad Song Survey. I asked my readers to vote for what they considered to be the worst songs, the songs that cause them to poke finger holes in their car radios in their desperate haste to change the station.

The response was unbelievable. I think more people voted in the Bad Song Survey than in the presidential election. Certainly the Bad Song voters were more enthusiastic. Here are some typical quotes from the voters:

- "The number one worst piece of pus-oozing, vomit-inducing, camel-spitting, cow-phlegm song EVER in the history of the SOLAR system is 'Dreams of the Everyday Housewife.'"

- "I'd rather chew a jumbo roll of tinfoil than hear 'Hey Paula' by Paul and Paula."

- "Whenever I hear the Four Seasons' 'Walk Like a Man,' I want to scream, 'Frankie, SING like a man!'"

- "I wholeheartedly believe that 'Ballerina Girl' is responsible for 90 percent of the violent crimes in North America today."

- "I nominate every song ever sung by the Doobie Brothers. Future ones also."

- "Have you noticed how the hole in the ozone layer has grown progressively larger since rap got popular?"

- "I nominate 'Cat's in the Cradle' by Harry Chapin. Harry's dead, of course, so we'll never have to worry about hearing it performed live again, but darn it, Dave, the next disc jockey here in K.C. that plays that song is going to get smacked across the head with a tube sock full of wood screws."

I ended up writing *two* columns on the results of the Bad Song Survey. These columns generated still *more* mail, some from people who wanted to cast additional votes ("I can't BELIEVE you left out 'Eve of

Destruction!' I HATE THAT SONG!"); some from people who were very upset about certain songs that were voted as bad ("Perhaps your readers are not aware that 'The Lion Sleeps Tonight' is a very fine traditional..."). And I heard from some people whose lives had actually been changed by the survey. Here's one of my favorite letters:

> Dear Dave,
>
> Your articles on Bad Songs were wonderful. I laughed 'til I cried. However, when I tried to read it to my boyfriend, much to my dismay he knew the words to all of the songs and *likes* them. I had to repeatedly stop reading so he could sing each one, and then listen to his exclamations of "What's wrong with THAT one!?" and "He doesn't like 'Honey'?!!!" etc. I knew he was a sentimental fool, but had no idea how bad his taste was. Now I'm afraid we're too incompatible to continue the relationship.
>
> Thanks a lot, Dave.
>
> Susan Bolton
> "Alone again, naturally"

And that was not the end of it. I don't think there will *ever* be an end to it. We've had an entire presidential administration[2] since the Bad Song Survey, and I am *still* getting mail about it from people wishing to vote for songs they hate, as well as from fans whom I have offended.

Special Note to Neil Diamond Fans

Please stop writing! You have convinced me! Neil is a music god! I worship Neil on a daily basis at a tasteful shrine to him erected in my living room! I love *all* the songs Neil sang to us! Not to mention all the songs he brang to us!

Why do people feel so passionate about this subject? Because music is *personal*. The songs we hear a lot—particularly the ones we hear when we're young—soak into our psyche, so that forever after, when we hear certain songs, we experience sudden and uncontrollable memory spasms taking us back to specific times—some good, some bad—in our lives.

For example, I cannot hear a Beach Boys car song

---

[2] If you want to call it that.

without being immediately transported back to the summers of 1962 through 1965. These were good summers for me—I was in high school and had never heard of gum disease—and Beach Boys car songs got played on the radio all the time, and I have loved them uncritically ever since. To this day, when I'm alone in my car, if the radio plays "Shut Down," a song about two guys drag racing—one driving a Corvette Stingray and the other driving a Dodge with a 413 engine[3]—I'll crank the volume all the way up and sing along:

Pedal's to the floor, hear his dual quads drink
And now the 413's lead is startin' to shrink

On a technical level, I have no idea what the Beach Boys mean by the term *dual quads*. I'm not a car guy. I'm the kind of guy who, if there's a warning light on my dashboard that won't go away, will repair it by putting a piece of duct tape over it.

But that doesn't matter. What matters is that when I'm singing along to "Shut Down," I'm no longer a middle-aged guy driving to the laundry to pick up my

---

[3] Whatever the hell *that* means.

shirts; I'm seventeen, and it's a summer night with tantalizing possibilities of adventure and romance hanging semipalpably in the humid air, and I'm cruising the roads around Armonk, New York, and even though the vehicle I'm cruising in is my mom's Plymouth Valiant station wagon, which boasts the performance characteristics and sex appeal of a forklift, I am feeling *good*, and I am stomping on the gas pedal (not that this has any measurable effect on my mom's Valiant) and imagining that I'm at the wheel of a Stingray, singing triumphantly along with the Beach Boys as we roar past the Dodge 413:

> *He's hot with ram induction, but it's understood*
> *I got a fuel-injected engine sittin' under my hood*
> *Shut it off, shut it off*
> *Buddy now I SHUT YOU DOWN!*

So I don't care how many times I hear "Shut Down," or "Little Deuce Coupe," or "Fun, Fun, Fun." They're always welcome on my radio; I'll go back to that summer night any time. On the other hand, I've always had a violent hatred for "I Got You Babe" because when it came out back in 1965 it was presented as some kind of anthem that spoke for America's youth; whereas in fact it was a flagrantly inane song ("So put your little hand in mine; there ain't no hill or mountain we can't climb"), on top of which, as an American youth, I did not wish to be spoken for by a whining little puke like Sonny Bono.

So songs evoke powerful emotions, both positive and negative. I think the negative ones tend to be stronger because, as I noted in the preintroduction warning to this book, your brain, as part of its lifelong effort to drive you insane, insists on remembering the songs you hate and playing them over and over and over.

That's why people still write and talk to me about the Bad Song Survey. They seem to have this powerful need to get their feelings about certain songs out into the open; somehow, this makes them feel better. It's kind of like psychotherapy, where the goal is to get patients to probe their subconscious minds, deeper and deeper, until they finally realize that the root of all their emotional problems is the fact that, during early childhood, they were exposed to the hit song "The Name Game" by Shirley Ellis ("Shirley Shirley bo Birley, bo nana fana fo Firley, fee fie mo Mirley, Shirley!").

Anyway, for whatever sick, masochistic reason,

people have been bugging me for years to write more about the Bad Song Survey. Okay, people—you asked for it. In this book, you'll find the survey results presented in far greater detail than in the original columns, along with many more bad songs and comments from the over ten thousand people who responded to the survey.

Before we get to the survey results, however, I want to stress a couple of points. The main one is that this survey does NOT attempt to cover all songs ever written. It basically covers pop and rock songs that were popular in the United States from roughly 1960 through 1990 because this is the era that shaped what is left of the brains of the vast majority of the people who responded.

There were some votes for older songs, especially the schmaltz-o-rama songs of the 1950s, such as "Oh, My Papa," "How Much Is That Doggie in the Window," and "That's Amore" ("When the moon hits your eye like a big pizza pie, that's amore!"). There were a couple of votes for "anything by Wagner." And there was one response from an opera fan who admitted that many impressive-sounding operatic lyrics become pretty stupid when translated into English:

BARITONE:	*Say you love me!*
	Say you love me!
SOPRANO:	*I love you.*
BARITONE:	*Oh! I'm so happy!*

There were quite a few Bad Song Survey votes for rap music in general, but virtually none for any specific rap song, perhaps because it is very difficult, even with sensitive laboratory instruments, to distinguish one rap song from another.[4] And obviously, since the survey was conducted in 1992, there are no votes for songs that have become popular since then. I think this is okay; to qualify as *really* bad, I think a song has to be sincerely hated by a lot of people for a minimum of five years.

Also, I arbitrarily ruled out certain songs, even if they got a lot of votes. For example, many people voted for two legendary songs by The Rivingtons, "Papa-Oom-Mow-Mow" ("Papa-oom-mow-mow, papa-oom-mow-mow") and "The Bird's the Word" ("The bird bird bird, bird is the word"). These songs are bad, yes, but The

---

[4] I realize this statement makes me sound like an old fart, but in many ways I *am* an old fart.

Rivingtons were obviously *trying* to be bad, and they succeeded spectacularly, which means these songs are *good*. For a song to qualify as truly bad, the artist had to be trying, on at least some level, to be good.

For this reason I ruled out the novelty songs that are clearly intended as jokes, such as "The Purple People Eater," "Itsy Bitsy Teenie Weenie Yellow Polkadot Bikini," "Short Shorts," "Alley-Oop," "Does Your Chewing Gum Lose Its Flavor (on the Bedpost Overnight)," "Transfusion," "Monster Mash," "Grandma Got Run over by a Reindeer," and "The Ballad of the Green Berets."[5]

Using similar reasoning, I ruled out the whole enormous category of country music, which has a long-standing tradition of songs with deliberately comical titles ("Drop Kick Me Jesus Through the Goal Posts of Life"; "I've Got Tears in My Ears from Lyin' on My Back While I Cry in My Bed over You"; "The Only Ring You Gave Me Was the One around the Tub"; "Take the Dice Away from the Baby, Momma, Before He Craps All over the Floor"; "Get Off the Stove Grandma, You're Too Old to Ride the Range"; etc.).

---

[5] This guy was kidding, right?

So I'm not saying this book is a definitive list of all the bad songs ever: It's just a bunch of arbitrarily selected ones from a survey of my readers, bless their twisted little minds. But believe me, there are *plenty* of bad songs in here. In researching this book, I spent weeks squatting on the floor, sifting through huge mounds of survey-response postcards, virtually every one of which triggered some god-awful song in my brain ("My boy LOLLIPOP! You make my heart go GIDDY UP!").

It was painful, but I did it.

I did it for *you*.

You you bo boo, bo nana fana fo foo, fee fie mo moo, you.

Bad Song Survey Results: The Big Vote Getters

"I don't think that I can TAKE it . . ."

I won't keep you in suspense. The worst song in modern history, at least in the opinion of the people who responded to the Bad Song Survey, is—better sit down and put your head between your legs— "MacArthur Park," the 1968 hit written by Jimmy Webb and sung hyperdramatically by Richard Harris. Come on now! Everybody sing along:

Someone left the cake out in the rain
I don't think that I can TAKE it!
'cause it took so long to BAKE it!
And I'll never have that recipe againnnn . . .
Oh NOOOOOOOOOOOOOOOOOOOOOO

Although there are many songs that I hate more than "MacArthur Park," it's hard to argue with survey respondents who chose it as the worst. All the elements are there: A long song with pretentiously incomprehensible lyrics that was popular enough to get a huge amount of air play and thus was hammered deeply and permanently into everybody's brain. Most of the votes for this song included some comment along the lines of "What the HELL is this song about?"

Naturally it turns out that there is a small but vocal group of people who like, even LOVE, "MacArthur Park." After the survey results were published, these people wrote me irate letters arguing that this song is a masterpiece and that the people who hate it do not understand that the cake is a *metaphor*. This is known, in legal circles, as the "metaphor defense." My response is, okay, maybe it's a metaphor, but it's a really *stupid* metaphor.

One of the people who voted in the survey, Lee Jones, told this amusing story:

> During high school, I played electric bass in the school jazz band. The night of the final spring concert, we were performing one of our band director's favorites, "MacArthur Park"—a song well established in the Pretentious Trash Hall of Fame. We get to the very end of the song, the band plays "BOM! BOM! BOM!"; the band director pauses to give the signal for the last crashing chord...George Roth, a senior trombonist, stands up (in the front row), slaps his forehead, and says, "Oh, Jesus! The CAKE!"

What I think really put "MacArthur Park" over the top on the Bad Song Survey Hostile O Meter is the fact that in 1978, just when it had started to fade from the national consciousness, it was brought back to life, Jason-like, by Donna Summer. This meant that in addition to the length factor and the cake factor, you suddenly had the disco factor. *Oh NOOOOO...*

Donna Summer also sang another song that got some votes in the Bad Song Survey; this is "Love to Love You Baby," which is about three hours and fifty-two minutes of Donna singing the words "I love to love you baby" and moaning like a person in the throes of either uncontrollable passion or severe intestinal distress.

Speaking of intestinal distress: The number-two[1] song in the Bad Song Survey was "Yummy Yummy Yummy (I Got Love in My Tummy)," the 1968 hit by Ohio Express. This is the same group that later did "Chewy Chewy," which is not to be confused with another much-hated song, "Sugar, Sugar"[2] which was performed by the Archies, who were so soul-free they made Ohio Express sound like Wilson Pickett. The

---

[1] Rim shot.

[2] There might be something about the word *sugar* because there was also a strong Bad Song Survey vote for "Sugar Shack."

Archies and Ohio Express, along with such bands as 1910 Fruitgum Company (perpetrators of "Simon Says"), were part of a genre of music known as "bubble gum," which gets its name from the fact that many people would jam wads of used bubble gum in their ears to avoid hearing it.

"Yummy Yummy Yummy" is an excellent example of the bubble-gum form. It's a love song, a sensitive, lyrical expression of romantic yearning, a plaintive, passionate plea, worded thusly:

> *Yummy yummy yummy I got love in my tummy*
> *And I feel like loving you*

Talk about your poetry! What woman could resist?

One interesting fact about "Yummy Yummy Yummy" is that Ohio Express did *not* do the worst version of it. A much worse version—so bad that it is wonderful—was performed by actress Julie London. Her version is part of another distinct genre of bad music, Songs Performed By Actors Who Unfortunately Do Not Have Any Friends Courageous Enough To Tell Them That, Although They Might Be Good At Acting, When It Comes To Singing, They Suck.

If you want to hear some great examples of this genre, you should get hold of a CD put out by Rhino Records called *Golden Throats*, which includes William Shatner performing "Lucy in the Sky with Diamonds" and "Mister Tambourine Man"; Leonard Nimoy performing "Proud Mary"; Mae West performing (I swear I am not making any of this up) "Twist and Shout"; Eddie Albert performing "Blowin' in the Wind"; Sebastian Cabot performing "It Ain't Me Babe" and "Like a Rolling Stone"; and Jack "Dragnet" Webb[3] performing a version of "Try a Little Tenderness" that is guaranteed to void even the strongest bladder.

But getting back to the Bad Song Survey: The song voted the third worst—speaking of love in a tummy—was "(You're) Having My Baby," by Paul Anka, who is widely suspect of also being Neil Sedaka. Many people, in voting "(You're) Having My Baby," cited these touching and very tasteful lyrics:

> *You could have swept it from your life*
> *But you wouldn't do it*

---

[3] Jack was once married to Julie London. This cannot be a coincidence.

We should not be surprised that Paul Anka was able to come up with these words. Paul has been giving the world memorable lyrics since way back in 1957, when, in his hit "Diana," he sang:

I'm so young and you're so old
This my darling I've been told

In that era Paul also gave us "Puppy Love" (later re-recorded, needless to say, by Donny Osmond) and "You Are My Destiny," which contains this extremely perceptive observation:

You are my destiny
You are what you are to me

But if you want my opinion, Paul Anka's ultimate achievement, the one that puts him head and shoulders above all the other songwriters, with the possible exception of Mac Davis (see below), is "My Way." This song, which has become the international anthem of drunken untalented businessmen in karaoke bars, has some of the most classic lines ever written, including:

23

Regrets, I've had a few
But then again, too few to mention

And of course:

I did what I had to do
And saw it through without exemption

And let us not leave out one of the most inspirational images ever put to music:

Yes, there were times, I'm sure you knew,
When I bit off more than I could chew.
But through it all, when there was doubt,
I ate it up, and spit it out

Speaking of eating, the song that finished fourth in the survey, just out of medal contention behind "(You're) Having My Baby," was "Timothy," performed by the Buoys. It's a real tribute to this song that it got so many votes because it was nowhere near as a big a hit as the three songs that finished ahead of it. But "Timothy" compensates for its relative lack of exposure by being *extremely* memorable, in the sense that the singer of the song appears to be saying that he...well, he *ate* the subject of the song. Really. What happened, according to the lyrics, is that there was a mining disaster:

> *Trapped in a mine that had caved in*
> *And everyone knows*
> *The only ones left were Joe and me and Tim*

Naturally, in a situation like that, after a while people are going to get hungry, and they're not going to be picky:

> *Timothy, Timothy, Joe was looking at you*
> *Timothy, Timothy, God what did we do?*

The singer is somewhat vague about what, specifically, happened next, but you can draw your own conclusion:

> *My stomach was full as it could be*
> *And nobody ever got around to finding Timothy*

I think it's a real tribute to the tastefulness of the Buoys that they did not attempt to boost sales by entitling this song "Yummy Yummy Yummy, I Got Tim in My Tummy."

Here is a significant fact: "Timothy" was written by Rupert Holmes, who wrote and sang *another* one of the songs most hated by the Bad Song Survey voters: "Escape," also known as "The Piña Colada Song." This song tells the moving story of two people who are losing interest in each other, so each one independently decides to cheat on the other, and when they find out about this, *it brings them together.* They deserve each other! Have another piña colada!

Rupert Holmes definitely should get some kind of special achievement award because he also wrote and sang "Him," the song that goes:

Him! Him! HIM
Whatcha gonna do about him?
You're gonna have to do without him
Or do without me! Me! ME!
No one's gonna get it for free
It's me or it's him

I don't know about you, but I would pick him.

Moving on with the survey: After the four leaders—"MacArthur Park," "Yummy Yummy Yummy," "(You're) Having My Baby," and "Timothy"—came a clump of songs that all got about the same number of votes. One of these is the Starland Vocal Band's "Afternoon Delight," which, at risk of being deemed a weenie,[4] I will admit that I actually kind of liked it when it was popular, but which apparently produces a near-violent negative reaction in many people. So does Debby Boone's inspirational "You Light Up My Life," which inspires a lot of people to hit the radio with a hammer. (Debby's dad, Pat, also got a solid survey vote for doing the world's whitest version of "Tutti Frutti.")

A lot of people also said they hate the Village People's hit "Y.M.C.A," but I think a lot of people also still love that song, judging by the fact that whenever it gets played at a sporting event, half the spectators leap to their feet and start forming letters with their bodies. (I think a lot of people are unaware that the song is about men picking up other men.)

---

[4] For more on this, see the section entitled "Weenie Songs."

Also getting a very strong vote—particularly from high-school students[5]—was "Achy Breaky Heart" by Billy Ray "Take A Gander At THESE Pectorals" Cyrus. Technically, I should exclude "Achy Breaky Heart" from this book on the grounds that it's a country song, made popular by people who did a complex line dance to it. But I'm making an exception and including this song, for two reasons:

1. I want to set forth my Mathematical Theory of Line Dance Complexity versus Intelligence, which states: "The complexity of a given line dance is inversely proportional to the average IQ of the people doing it."

2. I want to share the survey response of Mark Freeman, who, in voting for "Achy Breaky Heart," said he wasn't sure, but he thought the lyrics went something like:

> *You can tell my lips*
> *Or you can tell my hips*

---

[5] The high-school students also really hated Right Said Fred's "I'm Too Sexy," the one where he informs you that he is too sexy for his shirt, his car, his oral hygiene appliance, etc.

That you're going to dump me if you can
But don't tell my liver
It never would forgive her
It might blow up and circumcise this man!

Another song in this clump—one that I warned you about at the beginning of this book—is The Captain and Tennille's "Muskrat Love," a tender, poetic, squeak-filled ballad about rodents having sex. The Captain and Tennille[6] also got some survey votes for their 1972 number-one hit record "Do That to Me One More Time," which begins with the words:

Do that to me one more time
Once is never enough
With a man like you

Is it just me, or does that sound to you like a *serious* criticism of the guy's lovemaking technique? I mean, she seems to be saying, "Yo! Romeo! That's ALL? You're DONE??"

---

[6] Another Captain and Tennille hit, "Love Will Keep Us Together," was written by — You guessed it! — Neil Sedaka.

But by far the most deserving song in the second-tier clump, in my opinion, is "Honey," a song so cloying and saccharine and smarmy that it makes "It's a Small World" sound like heavy metal. "Honey"—a song about a really sweet person named Honey who has been tragically taken away by the angels—was sung by the legendary Bobby Goldsboro.

One survey respondent, Adam Groden, wrote: "Why does everybody hate Bobby Goldsboro's 'Honey?' I hate it too, but I want to know WHY."

To answer that question, let's consider this verse:

She wrecked the car and she was sad
And so afraid that I'd be mad
But what the heck
Tho' I pretended hard to be
Guess you could say she saw through me
And hugged my neck

Memories like this cause Bobby to sing:

And Honey, I miss you
And I'm bein' goooooood

As survey respondent Tom Cashin put it: "Bobby never caught on that he could have bored a hole in himself and let the sap out."

(Another respondent, Richard Silvey, wrote: " 'Honey' is bearable if you assume that it's the Hell's Angels that took her away.")

Several readers, using Bobby Goldsboro as the prime example, proposed the theory that any song connected in any way with the name Bobby is bad. Here's some additional evidence[7] supporting this theory:

- Bobby Vinton, who sang—actually, whined—"Mr. Lonely" and "Roses Are Red."

- Bobby Vee, who sang "'Take Good Care of My Baby" and "Rubber Ball." ("Bouncy bouncy! Bouncy bouncy!")

- Bobby Rydell, who sang "Wild One" and—I will never forgive him for this—remade "Volare."

---

[7] For some of this evidence I wish to thank my friend and bandmate Al "Bobby" Kooper, who also performed with the Royal Teens on the original version of "Short Shorts."

- Bobby Sherman, who sang various songs I can't remember the names of, but I figure they were probably lame because his name is Bobby.

- Bobby McFerrin, who gave us "Don't Worry Be Happy," which I have long suspected was part of a giant plot to boost sales of Prozac.

- Bobbie Gentry, who sang "Ode to Billie Joe," a fun tune about throwing something off the Tallahatchee Bridge and suicide and just generally the joys of rural life.

- "Bobby's Girl," sung by Marcie Blane, who courageously proclaims: "If I were Bobby's girl, what a faithful, thankful girl I'd be." (For more on this musical genre, see the section of this book entitled "Songs Women Really Hate.")

- "Bobby Sox to Stockings," a song by Frankie Avalon about the time "...when a girl changes from bobby socks to stockings; and she starts trading her baby toys for boys..."

- "Me and Bobby McGee," which is actually a fine song when sung by Janis Joplin, but which is usually butchered by other people, although this has not stopped a lot of other people from recording it, among them repeat bad-song offender Olivia Newton-John, who also sang "I Honestly Love You" and "Have You Never Been Mellow," not to mention "Let's Get Physical," which contains the incessantly repeated line "Let me hear your body talk." As survey respondent Abby Goldstein put it: "I don't *want* to hear anyone's body talk."

- "When the Red, Red Robin Comes Bob, Bob, Bobbin' Along."

But the king of the Bobbys, as far as the Bad Song Survey is concerned, is Bobby Goldsboro, who, in addition to "Honey," gave the world "See the Funny Little Clown" and "Watching Scotty Grow."

Speaking of repeat offenders, guess who wrote "Watching Scotty Grow"? Mac Davis! Mac got quite a few survey votes for "In the Ghetto," "Stop and Smell the Roses," "One Hell of a Woman," and—above all—"Baby Don't Get Hooked on Me," which contains what some voters argued are the worst lyrics ever written:

> *Girl you're a hot blooded woman, child*
> *And it's warm where you're touching me*

(For the record, Mac rhymed this with: "You're seeing way too much in me.")

While we're on the woman-child genre, I should note that there was a large mass of survey-voter hostility toward Gary Puckett, of Gary Puckett and the Union Gap, who gave us "Woman, Woman," "Young Girl," and "This Girl Is a Woman Now." Some voters argued persuasively that these are actually all the same song.

But if I had to name the one song that seemed to generate the most intense hatred, per voter, I'd have to go with "In the Year 2525," the inexplicable 1969 hit by Zager & Evans—the song that sticks in your brain like a malignant growth; the song that consists of an endless string of upbeat lyrics such as:

> In the year 4545
> Ain't gonna need your teeth, won't need your eyes
> You won't find a thing to do
> Nobody's gonna look at you

One survey respondent, J. Raoul Brody, belongs to a group called the Society To Undertake the Preservation of Endangered Dumb Songs, or STUPEDS, which performs bad songs in public. Brody wrote:

We have been performing hundreds of dumb songs to dismayed audiences across the country (mostly in San Francisco) since 1980. For your information, our most heavily requested song is "Muskrat Love," although "In the Year 2525" gets the most pronounced negative response — we've never made it past the first verse, whereas we've gotten all the way through "Honey" once or twice.

Running a close second to "In the Year 2525" on the hostility-per-voter ranking is "I've Never Been to Me," by Charlene, which was recorded on the Motown — yes, *Motown* — label and in 1982 reached number three in the United States, despite lyrics such as:

I've been undressed by kings
And I've seen some things
That a woman ain't supposed to see

Not to mention:

I spent my life exploring
The subtle whoring
That costs too much to be free

Right! Whatever that means!

Right behind "I've Never Been to Me" in the survey was a song that ranks extremely high on my personal list of songs that I would rather undergo a tax audit than listen to: "Seasons in the Sun," sung by Terry Jacks. This is a song about a person who is dying, but not fast enough. It features lyrics such as:

> *The stars we could reach*
> *Were just starfish on the beach*

The words to "Seasons in the Sun" were written by Rod McKuen, who also wrote and sang "Jean." There was only one vote in the Bad Song Survey for "Jean," but it's worth noting, because it came from Jim Hijiya, who offered an excellent revision of the lyrics:

> *Jean, Jean*
> *You're young and alive*
> *Which beats being old*
> *And dead*

There were two strong finishers in the Bad Song Survey in the subcategory of Bad Songs Involving

Horses. One of these was "A Horse with No Name," by America, which many people cited because of the lyrics:

> *In the desert, you can remember your name*
> *'cause there ain't no one for to give you no pain*

I myself have always found "A Horse with No Name" to be highly irritating. I agree with the comic Rich Jeni, who says: "You're in a *desert*. You got nothin' else to *do*. NAME THE FREAKIN' HORSE."

The other highly unpopular horse song is "Wildfire," the song about a tragedy involving a girl who goes out searching for her lost pony, named Wildfire. This song is sung by Michael Murphey in such a way as to cause a lot of people to feel less than charitable (as an anonymous voter put it: "Break a leg, Wildfire.").

One survey respondent, Steele Hinton, wrote a very thoughtful analysis of what exactly is wrong with this song. He was particularly unhappy with the part that goes:

> *Oh, they say she died one winter*
> *When there came a killing frost*

Hinton wrote:

> This is a tragedy for them, of course, but not for the world—that's what natural selection is all about. One can of course freeze to death in a "killing frost," but no normal person or pony would freeze as a result of getting lost in the killing frost. Evidently Mr. Murphey is a Southern Californian, and imagines that a "killing frost" is equivalent to a "killer blizzard," with blinding snow, wind, hail, lightning, sleet, fog, and deep darkness. Actually, "killing" in "killing frost" refers to your flowers and garden vegetables, and when one is forecast you should cover your tomatoes that are green and pick your ripe ones. A killing frost only happens when the sky is very clear and starry by night and deep blue in the morning—a fine day, if you don't have tomatoes. Nobody ever got lost in one who wouldn't get lost in July as well.

This makes sense to me, although I guess the song wouldn't be quite as dramatic if it were about a girl running around desperately calling for her lost tomato, named Wildfire.

Here are some other songs that got mentioned a lot in the Bad Song Survey:

- "The Candy Man," performed by Sammy Davis Jr. — If this song does not make you root for nuclear winter, then you are not human.

- "I Am Woman," sung by Helen Reddy — Don't get me wrong: I am all for gender equality. That's why I feel that if a woman sings a song that has lyrics such as "See me standing toe to toe" and "I'm still an embryo with a long, long way to go," she should be criticized just as a man would, especially if she also sings a song called "Leave Me Alone (Ruby Red Dress)," which seems to consist entirely of her singing the words "Leave me alone."

- "My Ding-a-Ling," by Chuck Berry — Chuck gave us a whole lot of great songs, and for that we will be forever grateful. But we already know WAY more than we want to about his ding-a-ling.

- "My Sharona," by The Knack — If push came to shove, I would rather listen to Chuck sing about his ding-a-ling than The Knack sing about their Sharona.

- "Morning Train (Nine to Five)," sung by Sheena Easton. Her baby takes the morning train! He works from nine to five and then! He takes another home again! To find her waiting for him! Repeat!

- "The Night Chicago Died," by Paper Lace[8]—This song still arouses great hostility for both music and lyrics. Several voters especially objected to the line "Daddy was a cop on the east side of Chicago." As Yvonne Koyzis observed: "There IS no east side of Chicago; just an awfully, awfully big lake. Daddy would've needed scuba gear to walk the beat."

- "Does Anybody Really Know What Time It Is?" by Chicago—Yes! Time to pass a law against playing this song! Also "Saturday in the Park"! Also "25 or 6 to 4"! Thanks for asking!

- "Disco Duck," by Rick Dees and His Cast of Idiots—Other than the fact that a lot of people hate it, I don't know anything about this song. Which is fine with me.

- "Playground in My Mind," by Clint Holmes—This is the one that features an irritating child's voice singing:

---

[8] Paper Lace, making a bid for bad-song greatness, also recorded "Billy, Don't Be a Hero," but the hit version was recorded by Bo Donaldson and The Heywoods (see "Teen Death Songs").

My name is Michael
I got a nickel
Which doesn't actually rhyme with "Michael"

- "Tie a Yellow Ribbon Round the Ole Oak Tree," sung by Tony Orlando and Dawn—I do not wish to sound insensitive, but if we really want people to come home, perhaps we should not have this song playing.

- "Signs," by Five Man Electrical Band—I think this song will forever hold the record for self-righteous hippie smugness, if only for these lyrics:

    If God was here, He'd tell you to your face
    Man, you're some kind of sinner!

- "American Woman," by the Guess Who—On second thought, maybe *this* song will forever hold the record for self-righteous hippie smugness.

- "I Love You Period," by Dan Baird—This song features the lyrics:

I love you period.
Do you love me question mark?
Please please exclamation point
I want to hold you in parentheses.

These lyrics prompted Jeannine M. San Giovanni to write: "This song makes me sick to my colon. I'd like to kick the author in his asterisk."

• "The Wreck of the Edmund Fitzgerald," by Gordon Lightfoot—Talk about your party tunes! Just put this song on the stereo and crank up the volume; then sit back and watch as your guests suddenly realize it's time to leave! Survey participant Jennifer Loehlin, speaking for many, gave this reason for selecting this song as the worst ever: "Because it features, in addition to general sappiness and bad rhymes, the immortal line, 'As the big freighters go, it was bigger than most.' "

• "Wind Beneath My Wings," sung by Bette Midler—Survey voters particularly objected to the line, "It must have been cold there in my shadow." Debbie Shanahan noted that the title of the song "has always reminded me of the clever farting sound you could make with your palm beneath your armpit."

- "Norman," the huge 1961 hit by Sue Thompson, with the chorus that goes "Norman, oo-oo-oo-oo-oo-oo-oo-oo! Norman, Norman my LOVE!" To tell the truth, only a few people voted for this song, but I'm including it here because I happen to have a deep-seated loathing for it, which is why I can so vividly remember its elegant rhyme scheme:

> *Joey asked me for a DATE*
> *He wanted to TAKE*
> *Me out to SKATE*
> *But I told Joey he would have to MAKE*
> *Arrangements with Norman*

Lest you think that all of the big winners in the Bad Song Survey were lightweight, simpering, and/or pretentious pop songs, please note that there was also a heavy vote for the heavy-metal Iron Butterfly classic, "In-A-Gadda-Da-Vida." A lot of people wonder what the strange-sounding title of this song means. It means "This Song Is WAY Too Long."

I think a number of rock classics fall into this category. For example—and I know I'm going to get into serious trouble with the Led Zeppelin people for this, but I need to get it off my chest—I sincerely believe that "Stairway to Heaven" would be a much better song if they cut maybe 45 minutes out of it.[9] I also feel this way about "Layla" by Eric Clapton (both versions), "Free Bird" by Lynyrd Skynyrd, "American Pie" by Don McLean, "Taxi" by Harry Chapin, "A Whiter Shade of Pale" by Procol Harum, "Another Brick in the Wall" by Pink Floyd, and of course "Hey Jude" by the Beatles, some of whom are still singing the na-na-na part.

I know these are great rock classics; I'm just saying that after a while they get to be great *boring* rock classics whose primary musical value seems to be that they give radio DJs time to go to the bathroom.

I am not alone in my feelings about these songs. A number of professional musicians wrote to complain about what a drag it is when their bands get requests to play the longer rock classics, as well as certain other

---

[9] For example, they don't need the part about "If there's a bustle in your hedgerow."

over-requested songs. Tim Rooney, a professional musician for more than twenty-five years, proposed this list of the ten request songs that Top Forty bands hate most:

1. *"Stairway to Heaven"*
2. *"Proud Mary (Rollin' on the River)"*
3. *"Louie Louie"*
4. *"Stairway to Heaven"*
5. *"Proud Mary"*
6. *"Free Bird"*
7. *"Stairway to Heaven"*
8. *"Feelings"*
9. *"Stairway to Heaven"*
10. *"Stairway to Heaven"*

Rooney, who plays in a Portland, Oregon, swing-and-rock band called the Swingline Cubs,[10] also proposed a list of the requests most hated by bands performing at wedding receptions:

1. *"New York, New York"*
2. *"Cab Driver"*

---

[10] Yes, this band is named after a stapler.

3. *"New York, New York"*
4. *"Mack the Knife"*
5. *"Joy to the World (Jeremiah Was a Bullfrog)"*
6. *"Girl from Ipanema"*
7. *"In the Mood, a.k.a. Something Us Old Guys with No Sense of Rhythm Can Dance To"*
8. *"New York, New York"*
9. *"Bad, Bad Leroy Brown"*
10. *"New York, New York, and I'm the Bride's Father and I Have Your Check Right Here in My Hand So You Better Play It, Dammit"*

I think these are pretty good lists, except for "Louie Louie," which—despite the fact that it got some votes in the Bad Song Survey—is one of the greatest songs in the history of the world. Part of its greatness, of course, is due to the fact that for years everyone was convinced that, in the Kingsmen version, the lead singer was singing dirty words, when in fact we now know that he was not. He was singing "In-a-gadda-da-vida."

Weenie Music

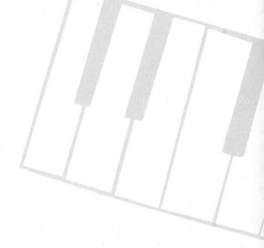

"I write the songs that make the
whole world nauseous"

What, exactly, do I mean by the term *weenie music*? I mean "The kind of sniveling, pouty, hypersensitive, self-absorbed song, usually performed by males, that makes you want to pick up the singer by his pencil neck and shake him until he stops."

A classic example of a weenie song—one that did very well in the Bad Song Survey—is Morris Albert's "Feelings," which gave the world this unforgettably eloquent expression of heartfelt emotion:

> *Feelings*
> Wo *wo wo*
> *Feelings*
> Wo *wo wo*

Probably the most violently hated of the weenie songs cited in the survey was "Sometimes When We Touch," sung in a very emotional manner by Dan Hill, who sounds as though he's having his prostate examined by Captain Hook. Voters were especially incensed by these lyrics:

I'm just another writer
Still trapped within my truth

and

I want to hold you till I die
Till we both break down and cry

Expressing a typical voter opinion, Laura Mc-Cusker wrote: "I always thought dentists should pipe this song into their waiting rooms. After sitting through it half a dozen or so times, patients would be BEGGING for root canal."

I think the same could also be said for another weenie classic, Bob Lind's "Elusive Butterfly," wherein he tells us that if we hear a sound, we should not be concerned, because it's only him, chasing "the bright elusive butterfly of love."

Yo, Bob: We're *not* concerned. Leave us out of it.

Of course when you talk about weenie music, there's one name you have to bring up, although I am very reluctant to do so, because on those occasions when I have said anything even remotely negative

49

about this person in my newspaper column, I have gotten an *extremely* angry reaction from his many, many fanatically loyal fans, so let me preface this with the following:

Special Note to Barry Manilow Fans:

Please do not get mad at me! I am merely reporting the views of other people here! I personally think Barry is the greatest! He is a music giant and a stud muffin of vast masculinity! I have a shrine to him in my living room! Even bigger than my Neil Diamond shrine!

P.S. to John Denver Fans: John is also the greatest! I don't think he's a weenie at all for writing "Annie's Song" and "Sunshine on My Shoulders"!

Barry Manilow got votes for several songs, including "Mandy," "Looks Like We Made It," and of course the truly hideous "Copacabana (at the Copa)," but he really scored big with "I Write the Songs." The irony here is, Barry DIDN'T write "I Write the Songs": it was written by Bruce Johnston,[1] and it was also recorded by (since we're talking weenies here) David Cassidy, who is also Donny Osmond, who in addition to "Puppy Love," recorded "Too Young," "The Twelfth of Never," and a number of other hit songs, despite the fact that he had, by actual count, over forty thousand teeth.

Another leading vote-getting weenie in the Bad Song Survey was Gilbert O'Sullivan, who was singled out for "Alone Again (Naturally)," in which he cheers everybody up with these words:

> *In a little while from now*
> *If I'm not feeling any less sour*
> *I promise myself to treat myself*
> *And visit a nearby tower*
> *And climbing to the top*
> *Will throw myself off . . .*

Don't let *us* stop you, Gilbert!

Other songs getting votes in the you-don't-love-me-so-it's-time-to-jump-into-the-bathtub-with-an-electrical-appliance genre were Eric Carmen's "All By

---

[1] Who, speaking of writing songs, also wrote "Do the Surfer Stomp."

Myself" and Randy Vanwarmer's "(You Left Me) Just When I Needed You Most."

In the Group Weenie Efforts category, the survey leader was Bread, which got votes for:

- "Diary"—"I found her diary underneath a tree and started reading about me."

- "If"—"If a picture paints a thousand words, then why can't I paint you?" (Huh?)

- "Baby I'm-a Want You"—"Baby I'm-a too lazy to write lyrics that scan, so I'm-a just add an extra 'a' whenever I'm-a need a syllable."

Another weenie band I'd like to take special note of is Climax, whose hit "Precious and Few" sounds roughly like this:

> Precious and few are the moments we two can share
> So it seems kind of odd that when we are together
> All I do is keep repeating the same statement,
>   namely
> Precious and few are the moments we two can share

With those precious words echoing in my few remaining brain cells, I think I'm-a stop here.

Love Songs

Words from the Heart
(Or Somewhere Around There)

L ove can be wonderful, but it also can be very destructive. It can cause people to lie, to cheat, to steal, to commit murder, and—worst of all—to write lyrics like these:

> *Why do birds suddenly appear*
> *Every time you are near?*

These lyrics are of course from the Carpenters' huge hit "(They Long to Be) Close to You," which received a solid vote in the Bad Song Survey. You frankly have to ask yourself: "Do I really want to be near somebody who causes birds to appear suddenly? Didn't Alfred Hitchcock do a *horror movie* about this?"

"(They Long to Be) Close to You" was written by Burt Bacharach and Hal David, who also wrote many fine songs. On the other hand, they wrote "Raindrops Keep Fallin' on My Head," not to mention "Wives and Lovers" (see "Songs Women Really Hate") as well as the Perry Como hit "Magic Moments," which contains these lyrics:

The way that we cheered whenever our team
*   was scoring a touchdown*
The time that the floor fell out of my car
*   when I put the clutch down*

But getting back to love songs: The voters in the Bad Song Survey singled out several songs that, although they seem to be intended to stir romantic feelings in a person of the opposite gender, seem more likely to stir some other emotion. Fear, for example. I am referring here to Steve Miller's "Abracadabra,"[1] which begins with this sensitive and poetic statement:

Abra, abracadabra
I wanna reach out and grab ya

A similar sentiment is expressed in the Four Seasons' "My Eyes Adored You," wherein Frankie Valli sings these classy lines:

---

[1] Steve also got a number of Bad Song votes for "Take the Money and Run," in which, in a single verse, he rhymes "Texas," "facts is," "justice," and "taxes." But we can forgive Steve for any bad lyrics he wrote because he also wrote "The Joker," thereby guaranteeing that thousands of years from now, people will still be wondering what the hell a "pompatus" is.

My eyes adored you
Though I never laid a hand on you

Speaking of romantic sentiments, one of my personal favorites, even though it got only a couple of survey votes, is "Girl Watcher," sung by the O'Kaysions, which features a line that would surely melt any woman's heart:

Hello there female
My my, but you do look swell

Gosh! Thank you, male! Let's have sex relations!

Another very romantic song receiving survey votes was Rod Stewart's "Tonight's the Night," in which Rod wins the Mr. Subtle Award for this line:

Spread your wings and let me come inside

In the same song, Rod also wins the Mr. Logic Award for singing:

Just let your inhibitions run wild

Don't worry, Rod! Our inhibitions are completely out of control! Which is why we're keeping our wings tightly folded!

A somewhat less direct approach was taken by Tony Orlando when he and Dawn sang "Knock Three Times," a song about a guy who is infatuated with the woman in the apartment underneath his, but he's apparently too shy to talk to her, so instead he sings to her, at the top of his lungs:

> *Knock three times on the ceiling if you want me!*
> *Twice on the pipe, if the answer is no!*

I hate to suck the romance out of this story, but there's a good chance that if Tony keeps *that* up, the neighbors are going to get some pipes and start knocking on *him*.

There are a lot more bad love songs, but in my opinion one of the worst, when you consider who wrote it, is "Silly Love Songs" by Paul McCartney because it . . . it . . . how do I find the words . . . it just *sucks*. And so does "My Love," wherein Paul, apparently too busy to write actual words, goes with:

Wo wo wo wo
Wo wo wo wo
My love does it good!

The big question is: What happened to Paul? Did his brain get taken over by aliens from the Planet Twinkie? I mean, he was a *Beatle*, for goshsakes, a certified *genius*, a man who wrote *dozens* of truly great songs, including such butt-kicking rockers as "I'm Down," and then for some mysterious reason he began cranking out songs like "Uncle Albert/Admiral Halsey," "Listen to What the Man Said," and "Let 'Em In," which expresses this powerful and universal theme:

Someone's knockin' at the door
Somebody's ringin' the bell
Someone's knockin' at the door
Somebody's ringin' the bell
Do me a favor, open the door
And let 'em in

Paul also got a number of votes in the Bad Song Survey for one line in "Live and Let Die": "But if this ever-changing world in which we live in..." Mr. McCartney, step up and receive your Certificate of Redundancy Certificate!

Not to keep picking on Paul, but, he also co-sang on another truly bad love song, "The Girl Is Mine," with (speaking of aliens) Michael Jackson. This is the one wherein Michael, needing a romantic, tender two-syllable adjective to describe the girl he loves, came up with:

> *The girl is mine*
> *The doggone girl is mine*

Fine piece of writing, Michael! Reminds me of Cole Porter! ("I've got you under my skin, doggone it!")

Michael Jackson was of course married for several sincere and meaningful minutes to Lisa Marie Presley, daughter of Elvis. The King sang all *kinds* of wonderful songs, including "Do the Clam," and in his early hit "All Shook Up" sang what I consider to be one of the finest expressions of love in all of music:

> *I'm proud to say*
> *She's my buttercup*

Yes, love is a beautiful thing, but when love goes bad, it can be a terribly painful thing. I will close this chapter by quoting from a song that, in the opinion of some survey voters, most eloquently captures this pain. The song is "Backfield in Motion," recorded in the 1960s by Mel and Tim, who conveyed the anguish, the despair, the loss, and the heartache of the jilted lover as follows:

I caught you with your backfield in motion, yeah
I'm gonna have to penalize you
Backfield in motion
Baby you know that's against the rules!

Songs Women Really Hate

"I Want a BRAVE Man, I Want a CAVE Man"

I decided to devote a chapter to songs that women really hate because—follow me closely here—the Bad Song Survey indicated that there are certain songs that women really hate.

A prime example is "Dreams of the Everyday Housewife," which was recorded by Glen Campbell and features these lyrics:

She picks up her apron in little-girl fashion
As something comes into her mind
Slowly starts dancing, remembering her girlhood
And all of the boys she had waiting in line.
Oh, such are the dreams of the everyday housewife
You see everywhere any time of the day
An everyday housewife who gave up the good life
    for me

BONUS POINTS: "Dreams of the Everyday House-wife" was also recorded by Gary Puckett.

Another song unpopular with women is "Little Green Apples," in which O. C. Smith sings boastfully about how he calls his woman up at home, "knowing she's busy," and gets her to drop everything and meet him for lunch, and he's "always late," but she sits there "waiting patiently."

BONUS POINTS: "Little Green Apples" was also recorded by—I am not making this up—Gary Puckett.

Then there's the 1969 R. B. Greaves hit "Take a Letter, Maria," the song sung by a boss to his secretary. This song prompted Denise Bernd to write: "As if she isn't busy enough, he wants to dictate a letter to his wife that he's leaving her. The guy makes my skin crawl. I'd love to hear Maria's response. Perhaps that's where 'Take This Job and Shove It' comes from."

BONUS POINTS: "Take a Letter, Maria" was also recorded by—I am *still* not making this up—Gary Puckett.

But the hostility for all of the preceding songs combined does not match the hostility voiced by women in the survey for Jack Jones's hit "Wives and Lovers," the one that goes:

Hey, little girl, comb your hair, fix your makeup
Soon he will open the door

Yo, Jack: Fix *this*.

Another detested song from the woman-as-helpless-appendage-of-man genre is "It Must Be Him," in which a desperate-sounding Vikki Carr sings something like:

Let it please be him
Oh dear God it MUST be him
Or I will stick my head in the oven again

And then there's "I Will Follow Him," in which Little Peggy March sings:

I love him! I love him! I love him!
And where he goes I'll follow! I'll follow!
    I'll follow!

" 'Cause I'm a moron," adds survey voter B. J. Halstrom.

AMAZING FACT: To the best of my knowledge, "I Will Follow Him" was never recorded by Gary Puckett.

Many voters cited various songs of teenage-female angst, with one of the leading vote-getters being Lesley "It's My Party" Gore, who was cited for the part of "Judy's Turn to Cry" where she sings:

> *One night I saw them kissing at a party*
> *So I kissed some other guy*
> *Johnny jumped up and he hit him*
> *'cause he still loved me, that's why*

Also cited by many voters was the Joanie Sommers hit "Johnny Get Angry." (I assume this is a different Johnny, but you never know.) In this song Joanie, in a giant stride forward for feminism, sings:

> *Johnny get angry, Johnny get mad*
> *Give me the biggest lecture I ever had*
> *I want a BRAVE man, I want a CAVE man*
> *Johnny show me that you care, really care, for me*

But "Johnny Get Angry" sounds like "I Am Woman" when you compare it to "He Hit Me (and It Felt Like a Kiss)," recorded by The Crystals, which features these lyrics:

And when I told him I had been untrue
He hit me and it felt like a kiss
He hit me and I knew he loved me
If he didn't care for me
I could have never made him mad
But he hit me, and I was glad

(We can only speculate whether O. J. had this on the cassette player during the Bronco chase.)

There were also survey votes for:

- Todd Rundgren's "We Gotta Get You a Woman," especially for the part where he sings "They may be stupid but they sure are fun."

- Kenny Rogers's "Ruby, Don't Take Your Love to Town," because, as Elizabeth Cosgriff put it, "In these days of kneejerk political correctness, it's refreshing to hear a song that's unashamed to stand up for wife murder." Kenny Rogers, by the way, gets bonus Bad Song points for singing, with Dolly Parton, "Islands in the Stream," which was written by the Bee Gees and begins with these unforgettable lyrics:

> *Baby when I met you there was peace un-*
> *known*
> *I set out to get you with a fine tooth comb*

- The Cornelius Brothers and Sister Rose song "Treat Her Like a Lady" because of the part where they sing "Strange as it seems, you know you can't treat a woman mean."

- And of course the lovely Willie Nelson/Julio Iglesias duet, "To All the Girls I've Loved Before, Please Send Me Your Blood Test Results Immediately."

Survey voter John Lilly nominated Billy Joel's "She's Always a Woman," with this explanation: "On first hearing, I thought it was a VERY long Geritol commercial ('OOOH, she takes care of herself...') and a damned good one, since it made me physically ill."

In conclusion, I would like to cite, as a strong example of the type of song that women generally do not sing any more as a result of the changing social climate, The Cookies' 1963 recording, "Girls Grow Up Faster Than Boys," which features these lyrics:

Won't you take a look at me now?
You'll be surprised at what you see now
I'm everything a girl should be now
Thirty-six, twenty-four, thirty-five!

I have to admit that, despite the lyrics, I like that song. I also really like another song done by The Cookies, "Don't Say Nothin' Bad (About My Baby)," in which the Cookies, standing up for their baby, sing:

He's good
He's good to me
So girl you better shut your mouth.

Say what you want about The Cookies; they were tough.

Teen Death Songs

GONE GONE GONE GONE GONE GONE!

Many, many voters in the Bad Song Survey felt that the worst songs of all are the ones concerning hormone-crazed teenagers who wind up going, through some tragedy or another, to that Big Prom Up in the Sky.

Although most of the classic teen death songs were produced in the '50s and '60s, this theme has been popular in music and literature for hundreds of years, dating back to when William Shakespeare wrote *Romeo and Juliet*, a play about two teenagers from enemy families who fall in love and try to run away, only to die in a car crash.

This is similar to the theme in one of the most famous teenage death songs, "Teen Angel," which received many survey votes. It's about a couple whose car stalls on the railroad track with a train approaching, and the girl gets killed. What makes this song *really* tragic is that it didn't have to happen. As the singer sings:

> *I pulled you out and we were safe*
> *But you went running back.*

The singer doesn't explain why his date had to be "pulled" out of a car that had merely stalled; perhaps she was an unusually large teenager who tended to get wedged between the seat and the dashboard. But the singer does explain why she "went running back":

> *They said they found my high school ring*
> *Clutched in your fingers tight.*

That's right: She placed herself directly in the path of a moving railroad train *for a high school ring*. Because of this, a lot of survey voters argued that "Teen Angel" is not so much a tragedy as it is an illustration of how the law of natural selection improves the gene pool. Nevertheless, I feel that, to prevent this kind of incident from happening again, we should all write to our congresspersons and demand passage of a new federal law requiring that the following warning signs be posted at railroad crossings:

THE SURGEON GENERAL AND THE SECRETARY OF TRANS-PORTATION have determined that if your car stalls upon the railroad tracks and somebody pulls you out, you should not go running back because this could be harmful to you as well as (if you are pregnant) your unborn child.

Another leading teenage car-crash death song is "Last Kiss," which was performed by J. Frank Wilson and the Cavaliers. In this song, the singer (presumably J. Frank Wilson) wails:

> *Where oh where can my BABY be?*
> *The Lord took her away from me!*
> *She's gone to heaven so I got to be good*
> *So I can see my baby when I leave this world.*

Frankly, if I were the Supreme Being, I would have a rule that you could not get into heaven if you had ever deliberately rhymed *good* with *world*.

The best version of "Last Kiss" I ever heard was sung by Stephen King, who's in a rock band, consisting mostly of authors, which I also belong to, called the Rock Bottom Remainders. (No, we have never made an album and for an excellent reason: We suck.) Stephen occasionally modified the lyrics to "Last Kiss." One time, describing the tender moment just following the car crash, he sang:

> *When I awoke, she was lying there*
> *I brushed her liver from my hair.*

If *that* doesn't bring a lump to your throat, I don't know what would.

Other motor-vehicle teen-tragedy songs include "Tell Laura I Love Her," sung by Ray Peterson. This is about a guy who enters a stock-car race so he can buy Laura a wedding ring, and *of course*, he crashes in a seriously fatal manner, but he still manages to sing "Tell Laura I LO-OVE her! Tell Laura I NEE-ED her!" approximately 153 times before finally shutting up. (I suspect that the ambulance crew turned off the oxygen.)

And, of course, there is "Leader of the Pack," performed by the Shangri-Las, which features a motorcycle accident (*VROOM* "LOOK OUT! LOOK OUT! LOOK OUT! LOOK OUT!" *CRASH*) and ends with the Shangri-Las singing:

> *GONE...*
> *The Leader of the Pack! And now he's gone!*
> *GONE GONE GONE GONE GONE GONE!*

Tragic-song teenagers do not always die in vehicle wrecks. Sometimes they jump in rivers. A good example of this genre is "Patches," sung by Dickey Lee, which is about a guy whose girlfriend, distraught that they can't be together, is found

> *Floating face-down*
> *In that dirty old river*

So naturally, the singer decides that he's going to handle this tragedy maturely and sensibly by *also* jumping into the river. ("Patches, I'm coming to you!")

The ultimate teenage-river-jumper song—and in my opinion, one of the worst songs ever made—is "Running Bear," sung by Johnny Preston. This is the song wherein background singers make what they apparently believe are Indian noises—"OON-gah oon-gah OON-gah oon-gah"—while the lead singer tells the story of Running Bear and Little White Dove, who belong to enemy tribes but love each other "with a love big as the sky" (maybe Shakespeare wrote this song). So they jump into the river and drown to resolve this problem and get away from the background singers going "OON-gah oon-gah."

One of the Bad Song Survey participants, Joan Kozlowski, said that when "Running Bear" comes on her car radio, "I just stick my head out of the car window and hope a semi gets it, just like my mother always said."

Sometimes the teenagers in these songs do not stay permanently dead. A fine example of this phenomenon is the song "Laurie (Strange Things Happen)," also sung by Dickey Lee, in which the singer meets a girl, lends her his sweater, and walks her home. The next day he goes back to her house to get his sweater, and the girl's dad tells him that *she died exactly a year before*. So he goes to the cemetery, and there, on the girl's tombstone, he finds—you guessed it—the high school ring from "Teen Angel."

No, seriously, he finds his sweater, and it is very thought-provoking. "Strange things happen in this world," the singer points out a number of times.

I want to close this chapter by revealing that I, personally, once wrote a tragic, teenage death song, called "Oh, Loretta." Unfortunately, it was never recorded, but I'd like to share the chorus with you here:

Oh, Loretta
Why did I let ya
Stand unattended
Near the threshing machine?

Songs People Get Wrong

Everybody Join In!

"A weema-wacka weema-wacka . . ."

One of the definitive characteristics of popular music, particularly rock music, is that the lyrics are often unintelligible. Of course, as we've seen in this book, this is often a good thing.

But it can drive you crazy trying to figure out the words to a song, especially if you like it. For example, I really like "Help Me Rhonda," by the Beach Boys, but I've never been able to figure out the opening lines. It sounds as though the singer is singing:

> *Well since she put me down*
> *There's been owls pukin' in my bed*

I hope these lyrics are wrong because if they're *right*, the singer's not going to get Rhonda to go anywhere *near* him.

Often the reason we don't know what the singer is singing is that the singer does not enunciate clearly. Elton John, for example, often sounds as though he's singing in a foreign language, possibly Welsh. James Brown routinely sings entire songs without making a single intelligible statement other than "Hey!"

Sometimes the problem is that the singer himself doesn't know what he's singing. As I mentioned elsewhere in this book, I sometimes play in a literary rock band, the Rock Bottom Remainders. As I also mentioned elsewhere in this book, we suck, but our musical director is an actual talented rock legend, Al Kooper, who at one time used to risk his reputation by playing with us. Al did one solo number—a long, slow, powerful blues song called "Caress Me Baby"—and although I understood all the other lyrics he sang, there was one line I could never get. Al sang it with what appeared to be tremendous passion, and it sounded like he was singing: "Goan rare-ro hah-dee-nah."

Finally, after hearing him perform the song dozens of times, I asked him what he was singing in that one part, and he said: "I'm singing 'Gonna railroad high tonight.' "

"Gonna railroad high tonight?" I asked.

"Yes," he said.

It turned out that Al didn't know what the lyrics were, either. He had listened repeatedly to the original recording of "Caress Me Baby," and the closest thing he could come up with was "Gonna railroad high tonight," and so when he sang the song, he just slurred that part.

For all we know, a lot of singers are doing this, which could explain why so many people have trouble with the words to certain songs. The example cited most often by people who responded to the Bad Song Survey was Bruce Springsteen's "Blinded by the Light." A great many people firmly believe that Bruce sings these words:

> *Wrapped up like a douche*
> *Another runner in the night*

Those are not, of course, the real lyrics. The real lyrics are

> *Wrapped up like a douche*
> *There's been owls pukin' in my bed*

Many people also reported that they could not understand the chorus to "The Lion Sleeps Tonight," which was a big hit for The Tokens. As you know, this is the song wherein the singer, after telling his "darling" to hush because the lion is sleeping, suddenly starts shrieking in a high, piercing voice loud enough to shatter crystal twenty-five miles away, while a chorus of deep male voices chants in the background, making enough noise to wake up a *dead* lion. Technically, the chorus is chanting the African word *Wimoweh*[1] but the Bad Song Survey voters who objected to this song—and there were quite a few of them—had many different interpretations of the lyrics, including:

> A *whemma weepa whemma weepa*
> A *weena whack a weena whack*
> A-wing go-way
> A-wing-a-WEP
> Ahweemowet, awheemowet
> Oh-we-mo-wet oh-we-mo-wet
> A *weema whip*
> Weema-wepah
> A *weem away*
> A-weem-o-wack
> Weema-wacka weema-wacka
> Wingle whip
> Weenie wrap

Speaking of weenies, many voters mentioned the song "Good Morning Starshine," as sung by Oliver;

---

[1] Which means, literally, "Yo no soy marinaro."

these voters definitely hated this song, but they were not at all sure how the chorus went. Among their interpretations were

Nibby nib nuby, nibby nobby nuby
Gliddy gloob glooby, nibby nabby nooby
Glibby glop gloopy, nibby nobby nooby
Yiby do diby, diby do bidy yadda yadda
Nibby nibby nibby, glibby globby glooby
Subba sibba sabba, subba sibba sabba,
* ho-ho, yo-yo*
Gliddy glup gloopy, oobie flobba noobie,
* lie lie, low low*
Glimmy glop glubby, wam alama looby,
* sha la la la low*
Nitty bloop bloopie, nibby nobby newbie,
* la la la, low low*
Ippy moopy wa-wa, dinky soppy da-da

There were also some votes for the sappy Wayne Newton[2] hit "Danke Shein," or possibly "Donkashane," or possibly "Dunkashein," or possibly "Duncashane."

---

[2] Speaking of whom: One survey respondent said that for years, when he heard Wayne singing "Daddy, Don't You Walk So Fast," he thought the words were "Daddy, Don't You Wash Your Pants."

Some survey voters' memories of certain lyrics were not 100 percent accurate. For example, there were voters who cited:

- The part of "Billie Jean" where Michael Jackson sings "The chair is not my son." (We don't know if this is the same chair that refused to listen to Neil Diamond.)
- The Procol Harum song about "Sixteen vested virgins."
- The Patti LaBelle song that goes "Voo lay voo coo shay, a vic mwa, cyst wa." (As we say in France: "Mare see!")
- The part of "I Am the Walrus" where John Lennon sings "I am the walrus, boo boo bi do."
- The beginning of "Annie's Song," where John Denver sings "You filled out my census."

Other voters had trouble remembering the titles of the songs they hated. We received votes for:

- "I'm Nothing but a Hound Dog"
- "One Toe over the Line, Jesus"

- "Goombayah, My Lord"

- "Shimmy Shimmy Cocoa Pops"

- "She Wore a Yellow Polka Dot Beguine"

- "Anagotalavita

- "The Wrapper"

- "Woodchuck Love"

- "Ain't No Woman Like the One-Eyed Gott"

- "One Ton Tomato" (The person who nominated this—and no, I don't think he was kidding—said it was a song "by some Spanish-speaking group" and that "all the words were in Spanish except the 'I ate a one-ton tomato' refrain.")

These are actually just a few of the many song titles and lyrics that people got wrong, but I'm not even going to try to list them all. Instead, I'm going to end this chapter, and then I'm going to—you guessed it—rare-ro hah-dee-nah.

Conclusion

I'm tempted to apologize to you, because if you have actually read all the way through this book, your brain is now an infected, festering, oozing mass of irritating melodies and pathetic lyrics.

But it's your own fault. I warned you, right at the beginning, remember? And you kept right on reading, didn't you? So don't blame me if, at this moment, the Greatest Hits of Mac Davis are echoing in your cranium.

Besides, it could have been much worse. There are a WHOLE lot of bad songs that aren't even mentioned in this book. For example, consider the lyrics to "Ball of Confusion," performed by the Temptations. The Temptations are without doubt one of the greatest singing groups ever, but in "Ball of Confusion," which is supposed to be a protest song, they sing, with great sincerity:

> *Great googa mooga*
> *Can't you hear me talkin' to ya?*

Now, those are some *terrible* lyrics, but they weren't included in this book. At least until now.

And there are many, many other bad songs that I left out. I know this. I know that—among many other shortcomings—this book barely even scratches the surface of the early work of Wayne Newton. But a person reaches a point where he simply cannot write about any more bad songs, and I have reached that point.

But before I leave you, I want to say a few things. First, I don't personally think that all of the songs in this book are bad. I actually *like* some of them, but I felt I had to include them if they got a lot of Bad Song Survey votes. So if I mentioned a song that you love and you're really angry at me and you want to track me down and kill me, remember this: I love that song, too!

Also, I want to say this to the many artists whose work was mentioned in this book: You should feel *good* about being in here. Really! Your presence in this book means that a large sector of the public still remembers your work! You made an impression; you made a *difference*. How many people can say that? Not many! Some really top musicians—and here I am thinking specifically of Handel—never wrote anything memorable enough to be mentioned in the Bad Song Survey. So I hope you respond to this book in a restrained and gracious manner that does not involve lawsuits.

Finally, let me say that music is *subjective*. There is no "good" or "bad"; there is only individual preference, which varies from person to person. If person A likes the song "My Sharona," and person B hates it, who is to say which one is right?

I am. Person B is right. "My Sharona" sucks. In fact, a tremendous number of songs suck, more songs than could ever fit in any book. And there are new ones coming along all the time. Even as you read these words, some young musician, somewhere, could be working on a song that will be *worse than any of the ones in this book*. Think of it!

And pray for nuclear war.

Credits

The following information was obtained from research and inquiries to those believed to control the lyrics from which the excerpts in the book were taken.

A. *Permission was granted for use of the excerpted lyrics from the following songs, and those giving permission requested that information about the excerpts be set forth as follows:*

1. Excerpts from "Wives and Lovers" first appearing at page 63, written by Hal David and Burt Bachrach, Copyright 1963 by Famous Music Corporation.
2. Excerpts from "Rose Garden" first appearing at page xiv, written by Joe South, believed to be owned by Lowery Music Co., Inc. Copyright 1967, renewal 1995.
3. Excerpts from "That's Amore" first appearing at page 13, written by Jack Brooks and Harry Warren, Copyright 1953 (Renewed 1981) by Paramount Music Corporation and Four Jays Corporation.

B. *Permission was granted for use of the excerpted lyrics from the following songs, and those giving permission did not give any instructions regarding how the information about the excerpts should be set forth:*

1. Excerpts from "In the Year 2525" first appearing at page 34, written by Rick Evans, believed to be owned by Zerlad Music Enterprises.

C. *Correspondence was exchanged with those believed to be the owners of the following songs. No agreement was reached on the terms by which permission would be granted. Therefore, permission was not granted:*

1. Excerpts from "Teen Angel" first appearing on page 70, written by Jean D. Surrey, believed to be owned by Acuff-Rose Music, Inc.
2. Excerpts from "Last Kiss" first appearing at page 72, written by Wayne Cochran believed to be owned by Trio Music Co., Inc. and Fort Know Music Inc.
3. Excerpts from "Yummy Yummy Yummy" first appearing at page 21, written by Arthur Resnick and Joe Levine believed to be owned by Trio Music and Alley Music Corp.
4. Excerpts from "Horse With No Name" first appearing at page xv, written by Lee Bunnell, believed to be owned by WB Music Corp and Warner Tammerlane Publishing.
5. Excerpts from "I Got You Babe" first appearing at page 11, written by Sonny Bono, believed to be owned by WB Music Corp and Warner Tammerlane Publishing

6. Excerpts from "Stairway to Heaven" first appearing at page 44, written by Roger Plant and Jimmy Page, believed to be owned by WB Music Corp and Warner Tammerlane Publishing.

7. Excerpts from "Wildfire" first appearing at page 37, written by Michael Murphy and Larry Cansler, believed to be owned by WB Music Corp and Warner Tammerlane Publishing.

8. Excerpts from "Wind Beneath My Wings" first appearing at page 42, written by Larry Henley and Jeff Silbar, believed to be owned by WB Music Corp and Warner Tammerlane Publishing.

9. Excerpts from "Young Girl" first appearing at page xvi, written by Jerry Fuller, believed to be owned by WB Music Corp and Warner Tammerlane Publishing.

10. Excerpts from "Rubber Ball" first appearing at page 31, written by Aaron Schroeder and Anne Orlowski, believed to be owned by A. Schroeder International LTD.

11. Excerpts from "Norman" first appearing on page 43, written by John D. Loudermilk, Copyright 1961 (renewed 1989) believed to be owned by Acuff-Rose Music, Inc.

D. *Permission was granted by one, but not all, of those believed to be owners of each of the following songs:*

1. Excerpts from "Magic Moments" first appearing at page 54, written by Hal David and Burt Bachrach, believed to be owned by Famous Music Publishing Corp and Casa David. Famous Music Publishing Corp. granted permission.

2. Excerpts from "Johnny Get Angry" first appearing at page 65, written by Sherman Edwards and Hal David, Copyright 1962 (Renewed) by Keith Valerie Music Corp, a division of Music Sales Corporation and Casa David, International Copyright Secured. All Rights Reserved. Music Sales Corporation granted permission and requested that the foregoing information be set forth as shown.

3. Excerpts from "Playground in My Mind" first appearing at page 40, written by Paul Vance and Lee Pockriss, Copyright 1971, 1973 by and Emily Music Corp. International Copyright Secured. All Rights Reserved. Music Sales Corporation granted permission and requested that the foregoing information be set forth as shown.

4. Excerpts from "Backfield In Motion" first appearing at page 60, written by Herbert McPherson and Melvin Harden, believed to be owned by Cachand Music Inc. and Patcheal Music. Patcheal Music granted permission and requested that the foregoing information be set forth as shown.

E. No response was received to requests for permission with respect to excerpts from the following songs.

1. Excerpts from "Tell Laura I Love Her" first appearing at page 73, written by Jeff Barry and Ben Raleigh, believed to be owned by Ben Raleigh Music Co.
2. Excerpts from "Ball of Confusion" first appearing at page 86, written by Norman Whitefield, believed to be owned by Jobete Music.
3. Excerpts from "I've Never Been To Me" first appearing at page 35, written by Ron Miller and Ken Hirsch, believed to be owned by Jobete Music.
4. Excerpts from "My Eyes Adored You" first appearing at page 55, written by Bob Crewer and Kenny Nolan Helfman, believed to be owned by Jobete Music and Kenny Nolan Publishing.
5. Excerpts from "Girl Watcher" first appearing at page 56, written by Buck Trail (Ronald B. Killette), believed to be owned by Drive-In Music Co., Inc.
6. Excerpts from "Lollipop" first appearing at page 16, written by Beverly Ross and Julius Dixon, believed to be owned by Edward B. Marks Music Co.
7. Excerpts from "Seasons In The Sun" first appearing at page 36, written by Rod McKuen, believed to be owned by Edward B. Marks Music Co.
8. Excerpts from "She's Always A Woman" first appearing at page 67, written by Billy Joel, believed to be owned by Impulsive Music.
9. Excerpts from "Land of 1000 Dances" first appearing at page ix, written by Chris Kenner, believed to be owned by Longitude Music Co.
10. Excerpts from "Feelings" first appearing at page vii, written by Morris Albert, believed to be owned by Loving Guitar Music Inc.
11. Excerpts from "Girl is Mine" first appearing at page 59, written by Michael Jackson, believed to be owned by Mijac Music.
12. Excerpts from "Do That To Me One More Time" first appearing at page 29, written by Toni Tennille, believed to be owned by Moonlight and Magnolias, Inc.
13. Excerpts from "Wreck of the Edmund Fitzgerald" first appearing at page 42, written by Gordon Lightfoot.
14. Excerpts from "I Am, I Said" first appearing at page 3, written by Neil Diamond.
15. Excerpts from "Play Me" first appearing at page 3, written by Neil Diamond.
16. Excerpts from "Love To Love You Baby" first appearing at page 20, written by Peter Bellotte, Giorgio Moroder and Donna Summer, believed to be owned by Ricks Music Inc.
17. Excerpts from "Alone Again (Naturally)" first appearing at page 51, written by Raymond O'Sullivan.
18. Excerpts from "It Must Be Him" first appearing at page 64, written by David Mack, Maurice M. Vidalin, and Gilbert Francois L. Silly, believed to be owned by BMG Music Publishers, Cedex, France.

F. Permission to use the excerpts from the following songs was denied.

1. Excerpts from "Abracadabra" first appearing at page 55, written by Steve Miller, believed to be owned by BMG Songs, inc. and/or Sailor Music.
2. Excerpts from "Johnny Get Angry" first appearing at page 65, lyrics written by Hal David, print publisher Hal Leonard Corporation, believed to be owned by Casa David.
3. Excerpts from "Magic Moments" first appearing at page 54, lyrics written by Hal David, print publisher Hal Leonard Corporation, believed to be owned by Casa David and Famous Music Corp.
4. Excerpts from "(They Long To Be) Close To You" first appearing at page 54, written by Hall David and Burt Bacharach, print publisher Hal Leonard Corporation, believed to be owned by Casa David and New Hidden Valley Music.
5. Excerpts from "I am Woman" first appearing at page 39, written by Helen Reddy and Ray Burton, believed to be owned by Irving Music.
6. Excerpts from "Shut Down" first appearing at page 10, written by Roger Christian and Brian Wilson, believed to be owned by Irving Music.
7. Excerpts from "Diana" first appearing at page 23, written by Paul Anka, believed to be owned by Chrysalis Music.
8. Excerpts from "My Way" first appearing at page 23, written by Paul Anka, believed to be owned by Chrysalis Music.
9. Excerpts from "You Are My Destiny" first appearing at page 23, written by Paul Anka, believed to be owned by Chrysalis Music.
10. Excerpts from "(You're) Having My Baby" first appearing at page 22, written by Paul Anka, believed to be owned by Chrysalis Music.
11. Excerpts from "Playground In My Mind" first appearing at page 40, written by Paul Vance and Lee Pockriss, believed to be owned by Emily Music Corporation.
12. Excerpts from "Signs" first appearing at page 41, written by Arthur Thomas, believed to be owned by Ensign Music Corp.
13. Excerpts from "Knock Three Times" first appearing at page 57, written by Irwin Levine and Russell Brown, believed to be owned by Forty West Music Corp. and Two One Two Music Co.
14. Excerpts from "Islands in the Stream" first appearing at page 66, written by Barry, Robin and Maurice Gibb, believed to be owned by Gibb Brothers Music.
15. Excerpts from "Him" first appearing at page 26, written by Rupert Holmes, believed to be owned by The Holmes Line of Records, Inc. and/or WB Music Corp and Warner-Tammerlane Publishing.
16. Excerpts from "Timothy" first appearing at page 24, written by Rupert Holmes, publication rights believed to be owned by Stanley Herman.
17. Excerpts from "Bobby Sox to Stockings" first appearing at page 32, written by Rus-

sell Faith and Clarence Wey Kehner, believed to be owned by MCA Music Publishing.

18. Excerpts from "Let 'Em In" first appearing at page 58, written by Paul and Linda McCartney, believed to be owned by MPL Communications, Inc.

19. Excerpts from "Live and Let Die" first appearing at page 58, written by Paul and Linda McCartney, believed to be owned by MPL Communications, Inc.

20. Excerpts from "My Love" first appearing at page 57, written by Paul and Linda McCartney, believed to be owned by MPL Communications.

21. Excerpts from "I Will Follow Him" first appearing at page 64, written by Norman Gimbel and Arthur Altman, believed to be owned by New Thunder Music Co.

22. Excerpts from "Honey" first appearing at page 30, written by Bobby Russel, believed to be owned by Polygram International Publishing, Inc.

23. Excerpts from "Laurie (Strange Things Happen)" first appearing at page 75, written by Milton C. Addington, believed to be owned by Polygram International Publishing, Inc.

24. Excerpts from "MacArthur Park" first appearing at page 27, written by Jimmy Webb, believed to be owned by Polygram International Publishing, Inc.

25. Excerpts from "Night Chicago Died" first appearing at page 40, written by Peter Callendar and Lionel Stitcher, believed to be owned by Polygram International Publishing, Inc.

26. Excerpts from "Running Bear" first appearing at page 71, written by J.P. Richardson, believed to be owned by Polygram International Publishing.

27. Excerpts from "All Shook Up" first appearing at page 59, written by Otis Blackwell and Elvis Presley, believed to be owned by Screen Gems/EMI Music Publishing.

28. Excerpts from "Baby Don't Get Hooked on Me" first appearing at page 33, written by Mac Davis, believed to be owned by Screen Gems/EMI Music Publishing.

29. Excerpts from "Bird's The Word" first appearing at page 14, written by Al Frazier, Carl White, Turner Wilson, Jr. and John Harris, believed to be owned by Screen Gems/EMI Music Publishing.

30. Excerpts from "Bobby's Girl" first appearing at page 32, written by Henry Joffman and Gary Klein, believed to be owned by Screen Gems/EMI Music Publishing.

31. Excerpts from "Diary" first appearing at page 52, written by David Gates, believed to be owned by Screen Gems/EMI Music Publishing.

32. Excerpts from "Don't Say Nothin' Bad" first appearing at page 68, written by Gerry Goffin and Carole King, believed to be owned by Screen Gems/EMI Music Publishing.

33. Excerpts from "Dreams of the Everyday Housewife" first appearing at page 6, written by Chris Gantry, believed to be owned by Screen Gems/EMI Music Publishing

34. Excerpts from "Girls Grow Up Faster Than Boys" first appearing at page 67, written by Gerry Goffin and Jack Keller, believed to be owned by Screen Gems/EMI Music Publishing.

35. Excerpts from "He Hit Me (And It Felt Like a Kiss)" first appearing at page 65, written by Gerry Goffin and Carol King, believed to be owned by Screen Gems/EMI Music Publishing.

36. Excerpts from "If" first appearing at page 52, written by David Gates, believed to be owned by Screen Gems/EMI Music Publishing.

37. Excerpts from "Leader of the Pack" first appearing at page 73, written by George Morton, Jeff Barry and Ellie Grenwich, believed to be owned by Screen Gems/EMI Music Publishing.

38. Excerpts from "My Way" first appearing at page 23, written by Paul Anka, believed to be owned by Screen Gems/EMI Music Publishing.

39. Excerpts from "The Name Game" first appearing at page 12, written by Shirley Elliston and Lincoln Chase, believed to be owned by Screen Gems/EMI Music Publishing.

40. Excerpts from "Papa Oom Mow Mow" first appearing at page 14, written by Al Frazier, Carl White, Turner Wilson and John Harris, believed to be owned by Screen Gems/EMI Music Publishing.

41. Excerpts from "Patches" first appearing at page 73, written by Barry Mann and Larry Kolber, believed to be owned by Screen Gems/EMI Music Publishing.

42. Excerpts from "Physical" first appearing at page 33, written by Stephen Kipner and Terry Shaddick, believed to be owned by Screen Gems/EMI Music Publishing.

43. Excerpts from "Tonight's the Night" first appearing at page 56, written by Rod Stewart, believed to be owned by Screen Gems/EMI Music Publishing.

44. Excerpts from "Treat Her Like A Lady" first appearing at page 67, written by Eddie Cornelius, believed to be owned by Screen Gems/EMI Music Publishing.

45 Excerpts from "We Gotta Get You A Woman" first appearing at page 66, written by Todd Rundgren, believed to be owned by Screen Gems/EMI Music Publishing.

46. Excerpts from "Sometimes When We Touch" first appearing at page 48, written by Dan Hill, believed to be owned by Sony ATV Songs LLC.

47. Excerpts from "Judy's Turn To Cry" first appearing at page 65, written by Edna Lewis and Beverly Ross, believed to be owned by Sony ATV Songs LLC.

48. Excerpts from "Muskrat Love" first appearing at page xviii, written by Willis Alan Ramsey, believed to be owned by Wishbone Music.

49. Excerpts from "Elusive Butterfly" first appearing at page 49, written by Bob Lind, believed to be owned by EMI Music Publishing.

50. Excerpts from "When the Red Red Robin Comes..." first appearing at page 33, written by Harry M. Woods, believed to be owned by Bourne Company and The Songwriters Guild.